THE CROWN OF THORNS

Gerald Davis

I finished your manuscript this morning –WOW!!
You have some massive revelation in these pages – I was really blessed by the Crown of Thorns prayer and the focus you brought to me of the associated healing—far crisper in my mind now than before.
I was also greatly blessed by your short explanation on Paradise and the work of Jesus from the cross to the throne – once again, far clearer than before.
I'll be re-reading this book and teaching several points for clarification in our services—what a blessing!

Thank you Gerald for sharing it with me,
Dr. Brian D. Scott - Canada

There is alot of wisdom in these pages. I am grateful to understand, for the first time, the redemptive power in the crown of thorns Jesus bore on the cross. Two types of people will love this book: those who value the sacrifice Jesus paid on the cross, - and those who want to live with the wisdom displayed by Daniel, king Solomon and Jesus.

Awesome truth!!
Sandino Castillo - Conroe, Texas

Not only is this a timely manuscript. - it is appropriate, easy reading, inspirational, edifying, thought provoking and Biblically Sound... we want to purchase the first 10 off the printing press...each one of my kids and grandkids will receive a copy... congratulations again!

Guy Worsham - Humble, Texas

It is wonderful to know the power that Jesus gave us through His persecution from the Crown of Thorns. Especially in a time where depression and mental anxiety is at an all-time high. This book confirms that every one of us can be freed from any oppression in our mind because of the Crown of Thorns that Jesus endured!

Dr. David Yanez – Kingwood, Texas

ISBN-13: 978-0-9904764-3-6

ISBN-10: 0-9904764-3-X

Library of Congress Control Number: 2014915703

Printed in the United States of America

RevMedia Publishing
PO BOX 5172
Kingwood, TX 77325

A publishing division of Revelation Ministries

www.revmediapublishing.com

Edited by Andrea Castillo

Dedicated To My Entire Family Down line

I dedicate this writing to our two sons, Jerry Ray and Tommy Van. Jerry is now pastor of The Embassy Church in Porter/Kingwood, Texas. Tommy owns and runs a money lending business headquartered in Madisonville, Texas.

I dedicate this book to their wives, Sally and Debbie.
Sally is Jerry's wife who also co-pastors the church with him. She and Jerry alternate preaching on Sunday mornings.

Sally is the newest daughter-in-law in our lives following Melinda's passing. What a wonderful daughter and grandmother she is to us and to our great-grandchildren. Tommy's wife, Debbie is a beautiful and very special lady who has been a wonderful wife, and mother of their three children.

I dedicate this book to our two grand-daughters from Jerry, and to their husbands,-

To Andrea and her husband Sandino Castillo, and their three little beauties, -Alyssa, Samantha and Laila.

To Tiffany, (Andrea's twin) and her husband Ray Lacelle, - and their three little beauties, - Lindsey, Rachael and Mindy. They live next door to each other in their new homes just about six blocks from Thelma and me, - yes, in our subdivision.

I dedicate this book to Tommy and Debbie's three children, and their companions, -To Crystal and her husband Shane Vance. They have two daughters and a son, - Brodie, Gracie and Madelyn. They are growing up too fast.

To Justin (my only sibling grandson) and his wife Casee, and their two sons Jace and Ryder. Their daddy is a world class roping star and they are coming along right behind him, roping everything in sight.

To Victoria, our youngest grandchild, and her husband Ash Karm. They have a son and daughter, Kashton and baby Makenna. We think she is our last.

God did fill up our quiver. I marvel at the faithfulness of our wonderful Heavenly Father.

Foreword

1st Corinthians 11:29 - 31 says: "For he that eats and drinks unworthily, eats and drinks damnation to himself, not discerning the Lord's body. For this cause many are weak and sick among you and many sleep. For if we would judge ourselves, we would not be judged"

My version; "Eating in the wrong manner brings hurt and harm, not blessing and health; - not discerning the Lord's body.

The CROWN OF THORNS affects the head; - probably the most important part of the body.
"Crown" = honor. Thorns = Hurt and Judgement
"Cross = The innocent one "made sin" for me. How could he love me so?

THANKS! - to such a noble undertaking. Calvary is ugly at it's Best!

No one that I know is more qualified to do this than my friend Gerald Davis, whose character and life declares the "cross" life.

WARREN J. PIERSOL

Warren Piersol was my wife's childhood pastor in Corpus Christi, Texas. This man gave me my first opportunity to enter full time into the ministry as a pastor in 1957. He is a very special man to me and to Thelma. He is now 93 years of age and has spent his entire adult life preaching the gospel of our Lord as a leader in his denomination. It is indeed an honor to have him comment on my book.

Introduction

I was raised in a family of preachers. We gathered every year for a reunion. I was taught about the things of God at home by a Godly mother and father who were both preachers, and at the reunions by the entire family of preachers. At one time there were about 23 preachers in the family. I knew very well why Jesus shed His blood, and by that shedding of Holy blood our sins were forgiven.

I also was taught well about divine healing procured by the thirty nine stripes laid on Jesus back from the scourge of the Roman soldiers whip. My father and older brother were both strong in the physical healing and miracle ministry back in the tent meeting days. But I never had heard anything about the PURPOSE FOR THE CROWN OF THORNS.

Something dropped into my spirit several years back that opened my understanding on this very painful part of Jesus' suffering. I began to share it in my meetings as a guest speaker, - and with some undeniable and remarkable results. After many years from receiving that insight, I share it now with you in this writing, along with some stories of the effects that I have experienced from sharing it.

Table of Contents

A CROWN FOR A KING

The crowd heard well when Pontius Pilate raised his palm, as he stood on his pedestal high before the mixed standing audience of people before him, many Jews and soldiering Romans, as he loudly declared "Behold Your King."

The company of soldiers proceeded to strip Jesus' clothes from him and hastily covered Him with a scarlet colored robe. He is a king, they mocked, so let's dress him like a king.

Then they twisted together a crown of thorns and set it on his head. They put a staff (a rod of authority) in his right hand. They knelt in front of Him and mocked Him; "Hail, King Of The Jews!" they chanted. They spit on Him and took the staff from his hand and used it to beat Him on the head again and again. After they grew tired of mocking Him, they removed the kingly robe from Him and put his own clothes back on Him. Then they led him away to crucify Him. (See Mt. 27:27-30)

Because we love the Lord like we do, it is not pleasant to think on this. It is especially not pleasant to write about it in such detail. When we do, we suffer with him in a measure. But we remember that the sufferings of our Lord were substitutional. He suffered so we wouldn't have to be eternally under the law, and separated from God because of our unforgiven sins.

I had never questioned why they would think to put a crown on Jesus head. He was a king. Pilate had openly declared that in his public announcement. Kings wear crowns. He was a king, He is a king, he is the "King Of Kings" and He is the "Soon Coming Again King." The soldiers shouted it in mockery, - we declare it in reality, in knowledge and in faith.

But why did they hastily make a crown out of thorns. Who ever heard of a person, especially a king wearing a crown made of thorns? Who, or what, was behind such an act? And what made a soldier go to the trouble of fighting with a poisonous thorny bush and twist it into such a device just to mock someone. No one ever in recorded history had ever worn such a crown, even in mockery. All other crucifixions' were committed for so-called "crimes done," and not in mockery. I've also wondered why the thorns were so handy and available for the soldiers at such a location? They were not in the woods where thorns might be handy.

But the question still lingers, - WHY THE CROWN OF THORNS?

THE THORNS

Thorns are poisonous. Thorns cause swelling. Thorns are painful. The mythical story of Androcles and the lion offers some meditation about the pain and discomfort that a thorn causes. The lion was so grateful for the removal of the thorn from his paw by Androcles, that he wouldn't eat Androcles when he was thrown to the lions for food, but instead protected him from the other lions.

THE HEAD BEATINGS

The referenced text records that the soldiers used the staff in Jesus' hand to beat him on the head "again and again". This is after they had put the crown of thorns on his head. Is it any wonder that Isaiah prophetically declared that his *"visage (facial recognition) was so marred more than any man - -"* (Is. 52:14). Obviously his face and head were swollen, both from the poison of the thorns and the beating of the stick on his head with the thorns, that he was almost unrecognizable. Undoubtedly there was bleeding from that crown of thorns circling his head.

THE THORNS

SEVEN POINTS OF BLEEDING

I have counted seven locations from which blood came during Jesus awful ordeal. The beating of the roman soldiers whip on his back. The hands and the feet where the nails were driven to hold him on the cross, - that would be five.

His side where the soldier drove the spear, - and then from the crown of thorns on his head. That is seven.

NO SPIRITUAL INSIGHT

Not one of the disciples nor his followers understood the spiritual meaning for why Jesus died. They only knew that the Jewish leaders feared that he would upset their established monetary system and their interpretation of Moses law.

Then also, their political standing with Rome would have been in jeopardy. We wouldn't even know today why Jesus died if it were not for the understanding and insight that God gave to Paul after his encounter on the road to Damascus. Paul spent two years following that experience all alone, by himself and the Lord in an Arabian desert. Paul learned from the Lord in some personal encounters with Him. Just as he did in his first experience with Jesus on the Damascus road, while he was in pursuit to capture and kill some Christians.

HOW AND WHY THORNS BEGAN TO GROW

Thorns are first mentioned in the book of Genesis as part of the curse which came as result of sin. All sin most simply stated is, - **VIOLATING THE INSTRUCTIONS OF GOD.**

When Adam and Eve responded to Satan's appealing and deceitful intrusion into their blissful life, in this place of perfection and unbelievable beauty, they violated the instructions of Father God and were removed from that perfect place to dwell.

When they made the decision together to agree with the serpent, they lost their protective covering. They unconsciously agreed that someone else was smarter, and more trustworthy than God. They were agreeing that Satan had more to offer than did God.

When they entered the human reasoning zone:

1. They lost favor with God.
2. They lost their intimacy and daily communication with God.
3. They lost their eternal life.
4. They lost their physical health.
5. They lost their prosperity as provided by God.
6. Worst of all they lost their ability to think like God.

THEY LOST THEIR MIND!

Now they can only function according to the way God's enemy thinks. When they were removed from the Garden of Eden the curse was released. That is what sin does. Look at the description of just part of the curse as it unfolds,

"Cursed is the ground because of you; through painful toil you will eat from it all the days of your life. It will produce thorns and thistles (weeds and hindrances) for you, - by the sweat of your brow you will eat your food."
(Gen. 3; 17, 18, 19)

"BY THE SWEAT OF YOUR BROW"

If God ever cries, he surely would have cried that day.

The growth of thorns clearly suggests the restrictions that man would encounter in his effort to make a living. Those restrictions show up in a variety of ways in our present lives. Paul referred to a difficult (complex) situation in his life by using the term "a thorn in my side."

People often use that reference to a situation they are dealing with in today's world. It is obviously an irritating and limiting something that just will not go away.

Every material thing that exists today came from the ground. Food, clothing. furniture, tools large or small, transportation, medicine and all the components and ingredients, etcetera. The thorns of some nature are still there to make production difficult to accomplish. Unrelenting determination is required to earn a living, - **because of the curse.**

It requires much study and meditation , much mental and physical muscle, to overcome the obstacles. As scripture records in Genesis; *"by the sweat of your brow shall you eat from the earth."*

ADAMS MENTAL ABILITIES

CONSIDER ADAM'S INCREDIBLE MIND

Observe the ability and description of the mind of Adam before sin entered the picture.

(Genesis 2:19,20) After the Lord God formed the wild animals, and all the birds,* He, (God) brought them to the man (Adam) to see what he would name them; and whatever the man called each living creature, that was its name. So the man gave names to all the livestock, the birds in the sky and all the wild animals."

INCONCEIVABLE

REALLY? If God could create it, Adam could create a name for it? And God was pleased with Adam's choices? Adam didn't have a language to draw from. Adam had to create a language as he needed it and be capable of coming up with a name for every species that God Almighty could create, and do it as God passed them before him. Evidently he had a mind that was equal to God except for the knowledge of evil. He didn't know how to dis-believe or question God. God gave Adam the authority to name everything He had made, and He then put Adam in charge of everything to run it on this earth. Whatever Adam called it, that is what God called it.

MY QUESTION?

Can you imagine dear reader, if that job was required of you? See footnote.*

Adam could communicate with God as a personal friend on God's mental level, - and he did it every day "in the cool of the day."

That continued until that dreadful day when Adam lost his mind.

Now he is more comfortable with God's enemy because that is the mental level he dropped to.

WHY WE STUMBLE

When we disagree with God we become uncomfortable in his presence. When we choose our friends today, we always relate to someone who has an IQ on somewhat the same level as we are. That is necessary for good friendship and fellowship. If we think like God's enemy, we "walk in darkness and not in the light." Then "we stumble at we know not what." (Pr. 4:18, 19)

God is light! He is omniscient! We think we know something. He knows that He knows! He is the father of all knowledge!

*There are innumerable species of both animals and birds Wikipedia estimates the number of modern day bird species to be between 9,800 and 10,500 species. The total number of non-bacterial and non-archael animal species in the world has estimates ranging from two million to 100 million. This would include fresh water dwelling animals and salt water dwelling animals as well as land animals both domestic and wild.

SICK HEADS AND FAINT HEARTS

I have discovered a description of the human mind as worded by God himself. This is what God said about human thinking after Adam thrust us into sin and disobedience. It is located in **Isaiah chapter 1:2-6.** God is in a lamenting mode here while talking through Isaiah His prophet to his people;

"- - I have nourished and brought up children, and they have rebelled against me." (An exact reference to Adam and Eve.)

Then he compares them to a dumb ox and a stubborn donkey. *"The ox knows his owner and the ass his masters crib: but my people do not know, my people do not consider."*

My paraphrase: "The dumb ox knows who he belongs to, and the stubborn donkey knows where he gets his food. But my people are not that smart."

"Ah sinful people - - laden with iniquity, a seed (from Adam) of evil doers, children that are corrupters: they have forsaken the Lord, They have provoked the Holy One of Israel unto anger, they are gone away backward."

My paraphrase: "You really amaze and anger me. You are traveling in reverse while you think you are going forward."

WORLD LEADERS

Many political leaders today are doing exactly that. They exclude God from their decision making. Their decisions are determined by their agenda and goals. To do the reverse of God's word, requires corruption, cheating, lying and deceit. It is like pushing a wet noodle. It just doesn't work. How can our head make a right decision when it is more comfortable in the absence of God? The choice to eliminate and separate God from any part of our life is a certain path to failure. A crash will happen, and they will always wonder why and they will blame it on someone else.

"There is a way which seems right to a man, but the end thereof are the ways of death" (Pr.14:12)

God's description of the mind of man continues;
"Why will you continue to be stricken? You revolt more and more: the whole head is sick, and the whole heart is faint."

Consider God's question in today's vernacular:

"- - Why do you choose to continue getting knocked down?

The more I try to teach you, the more you revolt against me and choose to do it your way."

What was their problem?

In the words of God Almighty;
Their "WHOLE HEAD WAS SICK!"

When the head is sick, the heart (soul of man) will be weak and full of fear. When the heart is full of fear, the mouth will utter frustration and negative sounds of defeat.

As Jesus said;
"For of the abundance of the heart his mouth speaks."
(Luke 6:45)

If faith in the word of God is there, the mouth will disclose it. If fear and wrong thinking is there, - the mouth will disclose it!

STINKING THINKING

Listen to the prophet as he continues to describe their problem; (Verse 6) *"From the sole of the foot even unto the head there is no soundness in it; but wounds and bruises, and putrefying sores: they have not been closed, neither bound up, neither mollified with ointment."*

My paraphrase:
"Because the head is sick, there is no soundness or wellness in the entire body from head to toe. Your wrong thinking has not been medicated properly, and the sores haven't been closed up; therefore you remain a stench in my nose."

Just God's way of saying; "Your thinking stinks"

Compare God's words in Amos 5:21-23, *"- - I will not smell your burnt offering and your meat offerings - - take away from me the noise of your songs; I will not hear."*

The mind wasn't right so the offerings stank in God's nose and the songs hurt his ears.

Question:

Did God not love them anymore? I know that was not the problem! They just didn't relate. They were not on the same page. They were not in harmony. They wanted God to accept their religious deeds while they kept thinking in reverse.

God was thinking forward, - they were thinking backwards. They were looking forward and going backwards with the "pedal to the metal."

APOSTLE PAUL

The apostle Paul struggled with his recognition of this problem.

"I find a law, that, when I would do good evil is present with me." (Romans 7:21)

Then He talked of a *"law in his members"* (the heart and soul) that was in constant struggle with the law of his mind (the spirit of man) that brought him into captivity *"to the law of sin and death."*

A TRIPARTITE CREATURE

Man is a tripartite creature – We are a **Spirit**, we possess a **soul** and we dwell in a **body**. The following verse speaks to that;

"May God Himself, the God of peace, sanctify you through and through. May your whole **spirit, soul and body** *be kept blameless at the coming of our Lord Jesus Christ."* (1 Thessalonians 5:3)

This is why Paul fought and struggled with this difficulty, and called himself a wretched (miserable) man. He agreed in his spirit that God was smarter than he was. But how does man align himself with God in his deeds? If I can't get my mind right, my deeds will never be right. All horizontal is determined by the vertical. If the vertical is not accurate, the horizontal will never be right.

IDENTIFYING BACKWARD THINKING

The following is a list of my observations about the backward thinking of fallen man:

-Fallen Man says: - **Thoughts of God are:**

1. I'll believe it when I see it. ~ **"Believe it and you will see it -"**
2. First come – first served. ~ **"The first will be last and the last will be first"**
3. I call it like I see it! ~ **"Judge not by appearances, but judge righteous judgment"**
4. I can't do that! ~ **"All things are possible to him that believes"**
5. I just don't have faith! ~ **"God has given to every man the measure of faith"**
6. I call it like it is! ~ God **"calls those things which be not as though they were."**

That is the way faith talks. God called into existence the things he wanted by his words. "Let there be light, and there was light," etcetera. If I always talk what I have instead of what I want, I will keep what I have and it will get worse. Satan will see to that! If I talk what I want, instead of what I have, God will see to it that what I want overcomes what I have, and things will get better. If what you have is not what you want, start talking what you want and see what happens. It is the way God thinks. (see Romans 4:17)

7. I doubt it! ~ **"only believe"**
8. That just makes me sick! ~ **"Himself bare our sicknesses"- "You will have Whatsoever you say!"**

(Jesus words) "Let the sick say
I am healed." Careless talk
will lead to defeated living.

9. I guess I will never be free!   ~   "He that is free in
Christ is free indeed"

10. I guess I'll never see the end of this!   ~   "surely
there is an end"

11. If I had it I would give!   ~   If you would give, you
would have it. - "give And
it shall be given unto you"

12. God, if you will bless me, ~ Do what I told you to
here is what I'll do.   do and I will bless you.

13. We are blessed to be a blessing!   ~ You are blessed
because you are a
blessing. "Them that
bless me will I bless"

"I will honor them that honor me!" Sow a seed, - then
get a crop! God says, - if you move, then I will move. God
is a good checker player, when it is our turn to move, -
he waits!

14. Well I know God can!   ~   "I will if you can
only believe!"

Faith says, "I can" – defeat says, "I can't." One is carnal – one is spiritual. One is the way God thinks – one is the way fallen man thinks.

"For as he thinks in his heart so is he" (Pr. 23:7)

God calls on us to move first and then trust him. **That is the faith life.** The unregenerate man wants God to move first, - then trust us!

A country song writer from years back put his thoughts about his departed sweetheart this way, "It's not her heart Lord, it's her mind; she didn't mean to be unkind, - why she even woke me up to say goodbye."

That speaks to us Lord. It's not our heart Lord, we love you! It's our mind, - we don't mean to be unkind, - we're just dumb!!Our carnal mind operates under "fallen man."

"My people (he is not talking about the devils people here) are destroyed for lack of knowledge" (Hosea 4:6) It is possible to be saved and go to heaven when we die, - and still be a loser in this life.

If I always think like I have always thought, I will always be like I have always been, I will always do like I have always done, and I will always have what I have always had.

We are moving toward the resolution of this issue.

THE RENEWED MIND

WHAT WOULD LIFE BE LIKE IF OUR MIND WAS
RESTORED?

**We are all familiar with educators of today who
assert that we only use about 10% of our brain
potential. How and when did that happen? Do you, my
reader, think God gave Adam that marvelous brain, and
then put a governor on it so it would only function at
10% of its potential?**

The best story I have ever found that illustrates what
it would be like to function with a renewed mind is
located in the first chapter of the book of Daniel.

HERE IS THE STORY

When Jehoiakim was king of Judah, Nebuchadnezzar,
king of Babylon came down and captured Jerusalem.

He seized the treasures of gold from the temple of
God to put into his temple. He authorized Ashpenaz, his
servant to seize the kings children and the princes. He
especially noted that he wanted only the best of them. He

specified those with the best personalities and who were the best physical specimens, smart and educated, who would not be an embarrassment to stand in front of the king.

He would teach them to learn the language of the Chaldeans. His intentions were to conform God's covenant people to their non-covenant and anti-God ways.

Does this sound familiar?

The king established a daily diet of certain meats and drink in an effort to make them the best they could be over a three year period. Four of those men who were captured were named Daniel, Hananiah, Mishael and Azariah. The kings appointed overseer promptly re-named them with Chaldean names. I will use the names most familiar to us of Daniel, Shadrach, Meshach and Abednego.

MAJOR FAITH CHALLENGE

When Daniel and the other three boys learned of the compromise they would have to make if they ate the kings meat, they commiserated.

If we eat the kings designated meat we will have to violate God's ordinance in Israel which commands us not to eat meat "strangled in blood." That must be respected. We will not eat that meat!

The Chaldeans didn't bleed their meat before they cooked and ate it.

•Our God is a God of principles. He taught us that the life is in the blood. You therefore do not eat anything strangled in blood.

•You don't yoke (plow) a donkey with an ox.

•You don't sow different kinds of seed mixed in the same field together.

•A man shall not lie with a man, and a woman shall not lie with a woman.

These things are a matter of principle, and are very important in the sight of God. While we understand that some of the old covenant rules have been modified under the new covenant in Christ, the first mentioned and the last mentioned above are clearly continued in the new covenant.

THE DECISION

What to do, they reasoned?

They wanted to be chosen for the best positions in the contest.

We may be captives in a foreign land, they reasoned, but God abides in our heart, wherever we are. He is the same here as he was at home. Let's try diplomacy first. Let's talk to Melzar, the chamberlain over this contest, and tell him that we want only veggies and water.

They knew it wasn't wrong to eat meat, but it had to be done in keeping with God's rules and principles. The exact same principle is true with sex.

Remember these words concerning Daniel;

(Verse 8) "—*Daniel purposed in his heart that he would not defile himself* —"(do something that would be out of line with God's approval)

God knows our hearts. I am convinced that it was Daniels resolve to stand firm with God's order of things that caused God to touch the chamberlain's heart with favor toward these men.

(Verse 9) "Now God had brought Daniel into favor and tender love with the prince – "

When Daniel, their spokesman approached Melzar with his request, the chamberlain was quick to listen, but was stunned. "Why?" "Just trust us for ten days", requested Daniel.

But Melzar feared for his life. "If I did that and you didn't turn out looking as good as the others, - the king would cut my head off."

There are quite a number of things in the scriptures that are matters of principle. Because our natural mind doesn't comprehend the full meaning of everything doesn't determine whether or not we should believe it. We first determine to believe the word of God, the BIBLE, - then we pray to understand it!

The limited and natural mind of man will never be able to think like God. That is so clearly obvious when we listen to many news pundits and interviews on television and radio. They can appear to be ever so intelligent with their use of an Ivy League education and the use of the most recent words and terms, but their views do not represent the mind of God. You have noticed how often the meaning of words are being changed. A word such as gay, - meaning "happy, in a good mood, or festive spirit," has now been changed by its continual reference, to mean the homosexual lifestyle. Another word used often is the word "disingenuous." It is obviously used to soften the term "lie" or "liar" or "hypocritical." There are several others commonly used in today's communications that changes the original use of the word. It is prophesied in the scripture that this would happen. The fallen mind of man appears to be bent on calling "good evil and evil good."

If you know the scriptures while you are listening to these terms, your spirit is getting a tilt, tilt, tilt. Men wink at sin, - God doesn't do that. God takes it serious! Our words reflect our hearts!

The scriptures are spiritually discerned as God gives revelation, insight and understanding.

We must learn to think by the Holy Spirit who always agrees with the Word of God. That is what is meant by *"walking in the spirit." "If we live in the spirit, let us also walk in the spirit"* (Gal. 5:25)

THE TEST OF COMMITMENT

"Prove us for ten days on veggies and water," Daniel challenged. *"Then look at our faces and our overall appearance, and compare us to those that ate the kings meat: then as you see it, you judge and deal with us accordingly."*(Verses 12 & 13)

Fearfully and reluctantly Melzar agreed to put it to the test for ten days. What followed requires some heavy meditation.

At the end of ten days their faces and bodies appeared healthier and better nourished than any of the young men who ate the royal food.

The results, after only ten days, is truly beyond anybody's expectation or understanding.

Only ten days? A week and a half!

What Melzar saw on inspection was a shock to him. It made a remarkable and indelible impression on him. How could just ten days on such a diet, veggies without protein, make that kind of visible and undeniable difference in appearance in these four men.

As I meditated this I had to wonder about that myself.

Melzar was so impressed at what he saw that he made a shocking decision. Contrary to the dietician's comprehension, this flew in the face of everything they had learned in their culinary schools. Still, to this day, this occurrence calls for supernatural allowance. It is not comprehendible to the natural mind.

Melzar thought it was the diet.

So he put everybody else on that diet for the duration of the contest.

This has to bring up a chuckle!! Three full years! Imagine the unhappiness, the grumbling and the whining of the Chaldean meat eaters.

Doing something God's way has to be a thing of the heart. It often doesn't make sense to the natural mind.

But then it doesn't have to. It is called obedience! And that is what God honors!

I know the diet is not what made the difference in these four men. All the other fellows ate the same things, - but they did not get these physical or mental benefits. These four young men who "purposed in their heart" to abide by God's rules, - clearly got supernatural help! Father, let that speak to us! These four Hebrews (keepers of the covenant) won the contest hands down.

THE AMAZING CONCLUSION OF THIS STORY

During the remaining three years of this period, the Hebrews were learning the Chaldean language.

Verse 17 may be the most fascinating statement of this entire story; "*As for these four Hebrews, God gave them knowledge and skill in all learning and wisdom: and Daniel (the one who had purposed in his heart to abide by God's rule) had understanding in all visions and dreams.*" **All three of these gifts mentioned are mental gifts. - Knowledge – skill in learning,** (understanding) – and **wisdom.**

When they stood before the king at the end of the three year contest they were obviously physical specimens.

The big tests were yet to come. How smart and knowledgeable were they?

The king had prepared a series of questions for all the contestants to answer. Not only did they excel in their mental gifting, but they did it in their newly acquired Chaldean language.

Now comes the single most astonishing comment in the entire story. This perfectly illustrates and defines the message we are considering;

"TEN TIMES BETTER"

(Verse 20) – "And in all matters of wisdom and understanding, that the king inquired of them, he found them **TEN TIMES BETTER** than all the magicians and astrologers that were in his realm."

Not ten times better than the dummies, but ten times better than the wisest, most educated and most gifted of any and all of the non-covenant contestants. They went from 10% brain power to 100% brain power.

Because Daniel could tell the king what his dream was, (spiritual insight and revelation) and answer an issue about the kings dream that was extremely troubling to him, which no one else could do, (can you say supernatural) Daniel and the other three covenant men were placed by the king at the top positions of leadership in the nation; only under the king himself.

JESUS

This brings to mind a statement made by some Pharisee's about Jesus after their effort to confuse Him, **"Never man spoke like this man"**

Are we making any progress here?

THE MIND OF JESUS CHRIST

"- - you seek to kill me, a man that has told you the truth, which I have heard of God: - -" Jesus words in John 8:40

I wouldn't attempt to exhaust this subject. No man could do such a thing.

In fact it staggers me to even imagine such an effort. I approach this only to establish how differently Jesus thought and therefore spoke.

Do you remember His words, concerning the words he spoke?

*"- - I do nothing of myself; but as **my father has taught me, I speak these things. (John 8:28)***

Again and again throughout chapter five of Matthew, Jesus used these specific words; "You say"- etcetera, "but I say"- and then he declared something different.

In Isaiah 55:8 God declared the peoples problem, **"My thoughts are not your thoughts, neither are your ways**

my ways, says the Lord."Our ways can never be God's ways if we don't first **think like God thinks.**

'FALLEN MAN' NEEDS A HEALING OF THE MIND

We have all seen the little bracelet, or otherwise applied slogan "What would Jesus do?"

While that is a noble approach to resolving a decision, it just doesn't work through natural reasoning. Our reasoning based on our knowledge level is not always reliable to determine what Jesus would do. When we read the four gospels we watch him do things on a daily basis that totally amazed the onlookers and left them speechless. Who would have predicted that he would do that, or say that?

Still today, after studying about Him for years we see and hear of things that God does that leaves us speechless and in awe.

Is it any wonder that national and world leaders disallow the name of Jesus and his words to be used in the secular world as our guide? Some pick and choose from Jesus words and spin them to help promote their anti-scriptural agenda.

"Oh, what a tangled web we weave, when first we practice to deceive."

They beat Jesus and mocked him, and nailed him to a cross roughly two thousand years ago because they **couldn't stand his words.**

The unregenerate minds of today still can't stand His words. If we quote him in a secular setting, we are ridiculed and labeled "Bible Thumpers."

Those dear unregenerate people have company, - **the devil hates to hear Jesus' words too.**

But His" - -*words of the wise are like goads – like firmly embedded nails –given by one Shepherd. Be warned my son, of anything in addition to them*" (Ecc.12:11, 12 NIV)

"JESUS NEVER FAILS!" "Heaven and earth may pass away but not one word spoken by Jesus, - has ever failed, or will ever fail!"

"A GREATER THAN SOLOMON IS HERE"

Sheba, queen of the south, rode a stinking, rough riding camel all the way across a burning hot desert just to see if a king in Jerusalem, named Solomon was "half as smart and wealthy and wise," as all the continual reports she was hearing from the traveling merchants declared him to be.

After a trip through Jerusalem they had all become rich. The reports were so consistent and steady that her curiosity could stand it no longer. This just can't be as they are saying. No man exists at that level. (See 1 Kings Chapter 10)

She approached Solomon with a list of heretofore unanswered "hard questions." The record shows that *"He told her all her questions, there was not anything hid from the king which he didn't answer."* (V.4 KJV) He even told her what her questions were. How could that be?

Answer: He was hearing it in his spirit - from God!

ELIJAH

Another example;

A prophet named Elijah, was being a thorn in the side of one of Israel's enemies. The enemy king was angry at his servants because someone was telling the king of Israel his secrets in planning war on Israel. "Who is telling him my plans" the angry king bellowed. "He knows what I am doing even before my army can put my plan into motion."

"A little bird tells the prophet Elijah the matter in his chambers, and then he goes and tells the king;" offered one of his subjects. That caused a lot of distrust and chaos among his subjects and soldiers. That king was ready to roll some heads.

Dear reader, Can you say "the Holy Ghost?"

SHEBA

Sheba was prepared to impress Solomon with a large caravan of camels, carrying gold, precious stones and spices, as her gifts to him from the south country.

She had heard much about his declared relationship with his God.

The merchants had talked about Solomon's unbelievable special approach when going up to the temple of his God to worship. Two hundred soldiers would stand face to face on either side of his path between the outer and the inner court, as the early morning sun was rising. Each soldier had a gold target almost as tall as the soldier himself. When the sun rose over the distant mountain to the east of Jerusalem, the sight was almost blinding. The sun striking the shields, and reflecting on the opposite shields, caused his path to light up in a brilliant golden glow from the outer court to the inner court, which could be seen by all viewers from outside, and above the walls.

Everybody under Solomon's reign was very wealthy. The scripture records that *"he made silver to be as valueless in Jerusalem as stones on the ground."* (v.27) Everybody had plenty of gold.

Solomon sat on a throne made of ivory. He then had it covered with the purest gold. Six steps wide enough for 12 lions to lay on, six on either side, ascended to his throne. Nothing compared to it in any kingdom known.

All the kings in the then known world, referred to him as the "The King of Kings."

After Sheba had seen the house he had built to live in, and the happiness of his servants, and the variety of meats and the setting of his tables, she had seen the lavish clothes that his servants wore, and all the cup bearers, (there was nothing but gold in all of his table wear, nothing silver), He then took her with him as he went up to worship.

In verse five, - it is recorded in these words;
" – *when she saw his ascent by which he went up to the house of the Lord, there was no more spirit in her.*" (V.5)

A LIFECHANGING EXPERIENCE

Sheba was dumbfounded and speechless. He then took her through his storehouses of treasures. He instructed his servants to watch her and listen for anything she said. When she commented on something that she was impressed with as they passed through his treasure houses, the servant was told to take it and put it into her saddlebags. She made this following confession to Solomon in these moving and unforgettable words;

*"- It was a true report that I heard in my land of your acts and of your wisdom. However, I did not believe the words until I came, and my eyes had seen it: and behold, **the half was not told me***: your wisdom and prosperity exceeds the fame which I heard." (V. 6, 7)*

She gave him all the abundance of jewels and artifacts that she had brought to impress him. What fascinates me is that Solomon put everything she brought to him back in her camel caravan, and gave her all the things she had commented on when she went through his treasure houses.

When she departed, she was not only at a total loss of words, she was far richer and definitely more wise than she had ever been. She had to have been 'in love' with him by now.

This puts me in mind of a song that I heard when I was just a child. The song was titled;

THE TRADE

- "I traded my sins for salvation
- I traded my load for relief
- I obtained peace for my condemnation

- and the joy of the lord for my grief
- I traded a life that was wasted
- for a temple to dwell that God made
- What I got was so much more than what he received
- I'm sure I got the best of the trade

JESUS REFERENCE TO THIS STORY

The doubting Pharisees stood in speechless amazement when they heard Jesus say, -

"The queen of the south - - came from the uttermost parts of the earth to hear the wisdom of Solomon, and behold, a greater than Solomon is here." (Luke 11:31)

They knew Jesus was referring to himself when he made that statement. They had not been able to confuse him or deal with his wisdom and teachings. They had been put to shame when they tried to catch him in some political statement or mistake. He always turned the tables on them and sent them away with their heads down and shaking.

But now, - to hear him say this!

But he said things even more baffling and astounding than that.

"Your father Abraham rejoiced to see my day: and he saw it and was glad."

They vehemently argued, "You are not yet 50 years old and have you seen Abraham?

Truly, truly, I say unto you, Before Abraham was, I am." (John 8: 56, 57, 58)

He was God with a fleshly body. He was the one who cut the covenant with Abraham. He created Solomon and taught him everything he ever knew. He created the worlds and the entire universe. He was the word of God, and by Him was everything made that was made. That is why He knew everything. He created knowledge. He knows every language spoken by man and angels. He understands all heavenly languages when we speak in tongues. He predicted all the coming events that we now see coming to pass. After two thousand years from his appearing, he is still the most talked about and quoted figure that ever lived. His words have outlived any argument that ever rose up against him. He promised all believers never ending life, even after the death of the body. He told us about the sacrifice of himself that he was going to make in order to make that happen. He promised us restoration to the Heavenly Father, and also life in abundance "now in this time." He would reverse what Adam had lost and get it back for us.

He promised to restore our minds and bring us back into communication with God.

THE RESTORATION PROCESS

"- - be not conformed to this world: but be ye transformed by the renewing of your mind, that you may prove what is that good, and acceptable, and perfect will of God" (Romans 12: 2)

There are three areas of human need. They are; **Spiritual, physical and material.** (3rd John 2)

We are a spirit, we live in a physical body, and we function in a materialistic world. If we don't have the material things necessary, the physical body dies. If the body dies, the spirit departs. Jesus spoke of production on three available levels. **30-60-100.** (Matthew 13:8) See above verse; **good, - acceptable, - perfect** will of God.

If you parallel that with the three areas of human need, you could say it this way;

One third of the benefits, (spiritual) two thirds of the benefits, (Spiritual and physical) or 100% of the benefits, (spiritual, physical and material.) Jesus was making provision to supply all three areas of human need.

It is possible to have only one third, or two thirds, or all three of the benefits.

If I believe for salvation through his shed blood, I can go to heaven even if I die sick and broke.

If I believe for supernatural health and apply my faith to the beating he received and the stripes he suffered, then I can have divine healing and health for my body.

If I believe for the material benefits that he promised, I can have all my material needs supplied when I believe and follow His instructions.

THE ISSUE AT HAND

Herein is the issue at hand;

Read again the opening verse of this chapter. *"- - be not conformed to this world:"* How do I escape that? In this same verse Paul is telling us how to escape being conformed to this world. We must, "have our mind renewed." Solomon made note of these three mental gifts. He explained them like this;

*"By **wisdom** a house is built, through **understanding** the house is established; through **knowledge** it's rooms are filled with all precious and pleasant riches."* (Proverbs 24 verse 3 and 4)

SUPERNATURAL MENTAL HEALING AND RESTORATION

Can I get that through this worlds education systems? No! We can't earn that any more than we can earn salvation. Learning the systems of the carnal and secular mind is not a negative. We need to learn all that we can. It helps us to know how and why others think the way they do. But take heed that it doesn't interfere with relying on the mental gifts of God. I would never send one of my children to a world system school that I knew would undermine the scriptures. Neither would I choose to go there myself.

Note Paul's warning concerning this potential problem;

"Beware lest any man spoil you through philosophy and vain deceit, after the tradition (culture) of men, and after the rudiments (pattern of thinking) of this world, and not after Christ." (Colossians 2: 8)

God's instructions will be simple and free from error;
*"A highway shall be there,- -the way of holiness; - - it shall
be for those: the wayfaring men, even fools, - - shall
not err therein." (Isaiah 35:8)*

And then Paul warns again;
*"But I fear, lest by any means, as the serpent beguiled Eve
through his subtlety, so your minds should be corrupted from
the simplicity that is in Christ."* (11 Cor. 11:3)

Warning from David in the Psalms;
*"Cease my son, **to hear the instruction** that causes to err
from the words of knowledge."* (Ps. 19:27)

Remember the above words of Paul;
*"- study (the word) to show your self **approved unto
God** - - ."* (1st Timothy 2:15)

I have come to understand and believe this: A person
must be willing to accept error by veering away from the
God inspired scriptures in order to be deceived. If I
"walk in the spirit", I cannot rely on my reasoning
abilities alone.

We cannot always rely on observation. We can't know
how God thinks unless we study His words. Natural

education will teach you how to function in the natural mind. To be "approved of God", we need to know how He thinks and then think and speak accordingly.

Godly knowledge, and wisdom, and understanding is a gift of God, which gives us the ability to see things the way God views them. This was purchased for us by Jesus, and then God gives it to us "by grace through faith." The scripture tells us that Jesus "knew what was in man." (1st John: 2:25) We need that kind of understanding.

Through Jesus work on the day of the cross, there is an atonement for obtaining these mental gifts.

Remember Daniel, Meshach, Shadrach and Abednego.

They obtained these mental gifts by an act of God. But they were under the old covenant. Those benefits were not available to the gentile world until Jesus opened up the way for all humanity. Now there is no difference between the Jew and the gentile concerning God's supernatural provision. When Jesus gave up the ghost and died on the cross, the scripture records that the veil in the temple, that divided man from the Holy presence of God, was torn from top to the bottom. (see Matthew 27:51). When that happened it opened up all of God's supernatural provisions to Him that believes. "Call on the name of the Lord and you will be saved." "To the Jew first" - and then to the gentile.

Saved from what?

1. From our sins that eternally separated us from God because of Jesus shed blood.

2. Saved from the curse of sickness and disease by Jesus stripes and physical beating.

3. Saved from a life of poverty because "Jesus became poor, (what we had because of sin) that we might through his poverty become rich." (2nd Corinthians 8:9)

4. That we might have a restored mind. "- - we have the mind of Christ" (see 1st Corinthians 2:16)

Now let's go to the provision!

THE PROVISION FOR A RESTORED MIND

JESUS' BRAIN

The sufferings of Jesus obviously included the crown of thorns. Reflecting on the previous notes about the thorns, there had to be some pain. Especially when the soldiers beat the thorns down into his head with that stick.

Why did the soldiers 'happen' to make a crown out of thorns? It was, without doubt, planned by God for a purpose. Surely that part of Jesus suffering had significance. He only suffered as a substitute on behalf of others. He certainly did nothing to deserve that.

Have you stopped to consider where that crown was located? It was placed around Jesus brain. **It circled His brain!**

If it was substitutional, then it did something for our brain, - if we understand it and believe for it?

Consider 2nd Corinthians 4:4;

"- -*the god of this world (Satan) has blinded the minds of them which believe not, lest the light of the glorious gospel of Christ, who is the image of God, should shine upon them.*"

Is any light beginning to shine for you here?

If you have believed to receive salvation through the shed blood of Jesus, by "grace through faith,"

If you have believed to receive healing for your body by the stripes and beatings on Jesus back, "by grace through faith,"

If you have believed to receive the Lord's favor and blessing on your finances because of your obedience through tithing and giving and following his instructions,

Then I offer you this truth about the healing of your mind:

The crown of thorns was suffered by Jesus for that purpose. The thorns, representing the curse that came on man through Adams disobedience; the thorns that caused pain and hindrance to mans ability to produce from the earth:

Those thorns (the curse) that represented the loss of our minds and separated us from thinking like God almighty, was removed from you the day Jesus paid the sufficient price on our behalf.

Again I say, as when the day man was removed from the garden - if God ever cried, it would have been on that day that He lost man's fellowship and man lost his innocence;

And then again, on this day, when he had to turn his back on his suffering, dying, perfectly obedient son and walk away.

*"Only let your **conversation** be as - - the gospel of Christ: - -stand fast in one spirit, with one mind, – for the faith of the gospel"* (Phil 1:27)

I am going to lead you in a prayer for the renewing of your mind. I am going to believe with you for a glorious miracle for the restoring of your mind. I want you to expect a change to come in your mental ability. **Before we pray** this prayer I want to share two testimonies with you of mental miracles, - and some thoughts and directives on how to "rightly divide the word of truth".

THE MIRACLES OF MENTAL HEALING

MIRACLE STORY ONE - LEARNING PROBLEM IN ELEMENTARY GRADE

I have shared this message in part with several congregations in my past traveling ministry. Roughly 25 years ago I shared the essence of this truth with a church congregation in Dearborn, Michigan. At the close of the message I asked everyone who needed help with their mental limitations to place their hands like a crown around their head, symbolizing the crown of thorns.

I then led them in a prayer claiming the crown of thorns, to remove the curse from the mind of man. Quite a few people joined me in that act of faith and prayer.

I then encouraged the people to go home and do this same thing over their children, and if possible over their grand-children.

When I returned about a year later I was introduced by the pastor to a mother, who told me following story. She also wrote it in a letter to me.

Her son, who was in the second grade, was having trouble in school with his lessons. He couldn't learn. He had much trouble with reading. His teacher had called and visited with the parents about the issue. The boy's name was Paul. His mother's name is Cathy. Cathy went home and did as I had instructed over her son. I called the pastor just before writing this story in this book, roughly 25 years after this occasion. I wanted to get an up to date report of this lad as the story stands today.

This is the report that pastor Tony, and his wife Jean just gave me about Paul.

Paul immediately began to change in his academic ability. His grades began to improve. His mother told me in her letter that the school had called to ask what they done to help Paul, remarking on how he had suddenly began to change in his grades. They wanted to know if they had obtained a special tutor. Today Paul has finished high school and gone through college, and is now a ranking officer in the navy.

Pastors Tony and Jean stated to me that they still today, give that taped message to people who come to them for counseling about their children's learning issues.

MIRACLE STORY TWO –HOCKEY TEAM

I had another case about a young man who wanted to play on the school hockey team. The coach wouldn't let him on the team because he "just wasn't coordinated." After the parents had followed my instructions concerning the crown of thorns, the boy was noticed by the coach as he was playing by himself on the ice. The coach called the boy over and asked him what he had been doing to make such improvement. The coach then invited the boy to come out for practice. As the story went, the lad not only made the team, but he became the goalie. At the end of the year he was named the MVP.

BY FAITH

Obtaining the benefits of Jesus work on the cross can only be done "by grace through faith." No one is required to believe. It is a simple invitation to whosoever will.

If we have to be convinced through the reasoning processes there will be many things that can stand in our way. Satan has a beguiling way of interfering with our faith.

One certain rule of thumb; -

IF IT INTERFERES WITH OUR FAITH, - IT IS WRONG, AND IS COMING FROM YOUR ENEMY!

An instant work of healing of any physical maladies in the brain can be received by the prayer of faith, when we apply the crown of thorns. Then the mental gifts can apply by the activity of the Holy Ghost living within us. The gifts of Wisdom, Knowledge and Understanding according to the thinking of God. That thinking develops as we "learn of Him," and study His ways of going and thinking.

The SPIRIT and the WORD always agree.

In the next chapter I will give you some thoughts of guidance on how to keep your thinking on track and not be "beguiled" by the enemy. There is always a ditch to avoid on either side of the road. You can become so negative and "prove it" minded that your faith can't work. Or you can become so removed from the judgment teachings of the word that there is no such thing as sin any more. The fact that there are so many varied doctrines among those who study the same bible, is proof enough that somebody missed the meaning of something somewhere.

RIGHTLY DIVIDING THE WORD

THE FOLLOWING ARE SOME THOUGHTS OF GUIDANCE ON HOW TO BETTER UNDERSTAND THE SCRIPTURES AND THINK THE THOUGHTS OF GOD.

Jesus is the only person who ever established a will and testament; - then lived a life to show how it is supposed to be done; - and then died to put the will into motion; - and then, to complete the process, he arose from the grave and lives to see to it that it is carried out right.

I will never understand everything in the bible. I have never met anybody who does. I keep getting insight and more understanding as I continue to study. You probably know that there are many differing views, and therefore many Christian denominations all teaching different doctrines. That of course causes division. That is not something promoted by God.

I have learned this; If you come across something that appears to be a contradiction in the scriptures, - it is a special invitation to receive a marvelous revelation of truth that has been hidden from you. But you will have to dig for it as for "hidden treasure." Supernatural revelation is just a step away.

Some things are deliberately hidden to be revealed in the future.

If a question comes into your mind while you are studying, it is not an invitation to quit or disbelieve, it is an invitation to learn something you didn't know.

Bear this in mind; "Every word of God is pure." He has committed himself to honor His Word.

The following are some rules that have worked well for me.

1. Instead of looking for errors, and there are some, especially when new translations are continually coming along, I make sure to concentrate on the intent of what is being said. **What is the message intended here?**

2. I also, mostly stay with the King James or the New King James. I understand that this translation from the original Greek and Hebrew language, was done under

the threat of possible death if anything was deliberately changed from it's intended meaning. Many new translations are corrupted with private interpretations that dilute the power of the word and undermine the spirit of revelation.

3. Also keep this in mind when rightly dividing the word of truth.

Following Paul's instructions to his son Timothy, in 2nd Timothy 2:15 *"Study to show your self-approved unto God, a workman that needs not to be ashamed (i.e.; - wrong, beguiled and defeated),* **rightly dividing the word of truth."**

4. The place to divide the First Covenant from the New Covenant (Old Testament-New Testament) is at the resurrection of Jesus. The New Testament doesn't begin at Matthew. The four gospels are listed in The New Testament, but no testament is active until the death of the testator.

Jesus is the mediator of the New Testament. In Hebrews 9: 15, 16 and 17 Paul says this about a testament;

"A testament *has no force until after the testator is dead."* (V.16) *"For where a testament is, there must also be the death of the testator."* (v.17)

Jesus lived his life, taught, ministered and died under the canopy of the first covenant. His ministry was to the Jews who had no revelation of any new covenant truths. At that time, no one did. They processed everything he said and did, by the letter of the law. His ministry was not yet sent to the gentiles. It is good to keep that in mind as you review the things Jesus spoke to them, as is recorded in the four gospels. The following is an illustration of what I am saying.

PARADISE: OLD COVENANT VERSUS NEW TESTAMENT

Before Jesus died and rose again, "paradise" was in the heart of the earth. Everybody who died in the faith, believing that the promised Messiah would come, had gone there into what Jesus called "Abrahams bosom."

It was located adjacent to the suffering part of hell where the wicked and unbelievers had gone.

A great "gulf separated" them. They had water and other comforts there and they had light. They were captives to Satan because of the law of sin in them. Jesus blood had not yet been shed for the remission of sin. This helps to understand the story that Jesus told of the "rich man and Lazarus." It was not possible for the blood of bulls and goats to remit their sin. Under the law, the sacrifices of those animals only covered their sin. They were held there in captivity until Jesus came and delivered them.

When Jesus died on the cross he immediately went to the "lower parts of the earth," - a place that Jesus called "paradise." Do you remember what Jesus said to the thief on the cross? "This day you will be with me in paradise."

The forgiven thief went there with Jesus that day.

Jesus preached to those in paradise concerning his work on earth, to restore those expectant believers to the bosom of God. They believed on him and he transferred paradise into the third heavens, where he presented his Holy blood to the father for the remission of all sins, both past and future. This happened during the three days between his death and his resurrection. The story of the rich man and Lazarus no longer defines paradise as it is now.

Eph. 4:9 *"- - before Jesus ascended, - - he also descended first into the lower parts of the earth."* He preached deliverance *"to the captives and led captivity (those held captive by satan) captive (to himself), and gave gifts to men."* Read Ephesians 4:8-13 and meditate. This could have only been known to Paul by divine revelation.

Before Jesus rose from the dead He transferred paradise from the lower parts of the earth to the third heaven.

Consider Paul's words in 2nd Cor. 12: 1-4, as he related a story of "a man who was caught up into the third heavens ..." Paul then called it "paradise." On this occasion sinful man had been forgiven by Jesus shed blood and restored to God. This incident with Paul happened several years after Jesus earthly ministry.

You can see how that Paradise was in a different location during Jesus earthly ministry than it was in the new covenant after his resurrection. Rightly dividing the word of truth requires study of the word of God. The more we study the scriptures, the more we increase in the knowledge of God and in the life of faith.

The teachings of Jesus concerning morality and a way of life and thinking are of course, for us to continue in the new covenant. But we are redeemed from the "curse of the law" through the price that Jesus our redeemer paid.

CLAIMING THE BENEFITS IN THE CROWN OF THORNS

A SPECIAL PRAYER FOR HEALING OF THE MIND

Please follow my instructions as we pray this prayer for a renewed and restored mind. A miracle is coming when faith is applied to this prayer. Place your hands around your brain. With your hands in that position, I strongly recommend that you say this prayer out loud. It will help to hear yourself speak as you pray this prayer:

Let's go;

Dear Heavenly Father – God of the universe – God of our fathers and Lord of heaven and earth, - I come to you in simple faith and in obedience to your word, - I need a miracle of restoration in my mind – I want to be changed from a mouth full of corruption and a head full of wrong thinking – I thank you for my salvation through the shed blood of Jesus – I thank you for His stripes that he bore for my physical healing – I now come claiming the "crown of thorns" placed around Jesus brain, taking away the curse off of my brain and off of my inherited, corrupted mind – I claim by faith

the miracle of mental restoration – I speak these words in faith as though I had already seen the answer – You, father God, cannot deny your self – your word is good – Jesus' sacrifice is enough – I cannot fail when leaning on your infallible word of promise – I no longer put my trust in the arm of flesh, - but my trust is in you. – Thank you for hearing my prayer and thank you for the answer – From this day forward I will be different – I will never be like I was before this prayer. – I say from my heart, it is different now; - right now! - Jesus, oh Jesus; - thank you for what you provided for me.

This verse from Isaiah 65:24 is for you, right now;
"And it shall come to pass, that before they call, I will answer; and while they are yet speaking, I will hear."

The spirit of weeping came over me as I worded that prayer. I know it is anointed of God.

Rejoice in your heart and praise the Lord for what He has provided, and for what he has just done for you!

Note: Put your hands around your children's heads, or your grandchildren, and pray a similar prayer over them.

Special Note: Do not offer a poorly worded prayer over your child. Write it down. Think it through! You want to say exactly what you are meaning to say. This is serious! This is not an act of hope alone. Do this in faith, - and believe for the change to come in this child's mental abilities.

THE TEACHER – next page.

THE TEACHER

THE HOLY GHOST

As time grew closer to face the crucifixion and the awful death that was ahead for him, Jesus was in a teaching session with his disciples, preparing them for what was coming.

He had told them that he was going away, and of course their hearts were filled with sorrow.

Then he told them something that they couldn't possibly understand.

In John chapter 16: v.5; He said this: " – *now I go away to him that sent me;* - then in verse 7 Jesus told them how the new mind would be put into motion. "- - *it is expedient for you (necessary for your sakes) that I go away: for if I go not away, the comforter will not come unto you; but if I depart, I will send him unto you.*"

"IF I DEPART"

Jesus' spirit departed from His body when He drew his last breath on the cross. He "gave up the Ghost". It was His Spirit that went into the lower parts of the earth during the three days his body was in the grave. Jesus spirit was reunited with His body at the time of His resurrection. Jesus spirit was the Holy Spirit! The Holy Ghost was the life in Jesus. Jesus was sired by the Holy Spirit, not by man. His mother was a virgin. The spirit of fallen man is passed on when sired by man.

The Holy Spirit was confined to Jesus body as long as Jesus was on the earth. If the disciples were to continue to learn of the benefits that Jesus had provided, they would need Him, 'the teacher' to lead them and teach them. That is why it was necessary for Jesus to go back to the Father and re-unite with Him. Then the Father could send Jesus Spirit back to dwell in the physical bodies of all believers. *"He dwells with you, - and shall be in you."* (See John 14:17) The same spirit that was in Jesus would now be in them. The 'spirit of man' would now be over-ruled by the voice of the Spirit of Jesus Christ now dwelling in you, - when faith for it is applied.

Here is the explanation of how this would work:
"- - When He, the Spirit of Truth (Jesus Spirit) shall come, He will guide you into all truth: for He shall not speak of

himself; but whatsoever he shall hear (of the Father), that shall he speak: and He will show you things to come." (John 16:3) Jesus is the Word of God, the Holy Spirit (Spirit of Christ) opens the written word up for us to understand.

When we study the word of God, in trust and not in doubt, the Holy Ghost will open the word up for you and help you to understand the thinking of God.

This is how we *"put off concerning former communication, the old man, which is corrupt - -."* (Eph. 4:22 and Colossians 3:9)

A humorous thought from a song writer says it like this:
"You gotta' know when to hold'em', and know when to fold'em'
You gotta' know when to walk away, and know when to run."
Isaiah said it this way:" *Your ears shall hear a word behind you, saying, This is the way, walk in it, when you turn to the right hand, and when you turn to the left."* (Isaiah 30:21)

*"This I say then, **walk in the Spirit**, and you will not fulfill the lust of the flesh.* (Galatians 5:16)

"If we live in the Spirit, - let us also **walk in the Spirit."**
(Galatians 5:25)

Some thoughts of guidance on how to **"walk in the spirit."**

1. Be sensitive to listen in your spirit.

2. He will speak to you when there is an occasion for it. He knows what is present and He knows what is coming.

3. Always be open and obedient to that voice inside of you. Your conscience will guide you concerning right and wrong when you know the word, - and when your spirit is open to listen.

4. The Holy Spirit is not a pusher. He will not force you to do right. He always leaves the power of choice with you.

5. When you don't know for sure what is the right move to make, talk in your heavenly language (tongues, the Holy Ghost language) and then take time to listen to your spirit for a period following.

6. God wants to guide you more than you want to be guided! Trust him to lead you when you ask Him.

7. Do your best, and then trust God to do the rest!

IN CONCLUSION:

My prayers go with everyone who reads this book. I pray that you will see the full manifestation of the power and
THE PURPOSE IN THE CROWN OF THORNS!

To use as addendum for further study

Also, other thoughts on the MIND and the CURSE and the BLESSING: Jesus was accused of being "out of His mind" – Mark 3.21 NKJV *(when it is we who before conversion that are out of our minds ;) The demoniac "sitting at the feet of Jesus, clothed and his right mind"* – Luke 8.35; *The Greatest Commandment to Love the Lord "...with all our mind..."* – Mark 12.30; *The "debased mind"* – Romans 1.28; *"set their minds on the things of the flesh"* ... *"the carnal mind"* ... *"the mind of the Spirit"* – Romans 8.5,7, & 27; *The "willing mind" and the "ready mind"* – II Cor. 8.9, 12; *The "Gentiles walk in the futility of their mind"* ... *"be renewed in the spirit of your mind"* – Eph. 4.17, 23; *"let this mind be in you which* *was also in Christ Jesus" – Phlp. 2.5; "who set their mind on earthly things" – Phlp 3.19; "And you, who once were alienated and enemies by wicked works in your mind" – Col. 1.21; "vainly puffed up by his fleshly mind" – Col. 2.18; "Set your mind on things above, not on things on this earth" – Col. 3.2; we are not to be "shaken in mind" – II Thess. 2.2; "God...has given us a...spirit of power and of love and of a sound mind" – II Tim. 1.7; "I will put My laws in their mind and write them on their hearts" – Heb. 8.10; "gird up the loins of your mind" – I Peter 1.13; "Here is the mind that has wisdom" – Rev. 17.9*

Special thanks to Rev. Cecil Barham for the added addendum